"No, silly!" chuckled Dad.
"The big pool isn't deep or cold. And the only teeth in it will be yours and mine! I think you're just feeling a bit worried. Are you?"
"I'm feeling a LOT worried!" said Lily.

You see, Lily had only ever been in the paddling pool. The paddling pool only came up to her knees.

But the big pool... well, she wouldn't even be able to touch the bottom without going underwater.

But if she wanted to learn how to swim... the big pool was where she needed to be.

"Listen peanut, I know it's scary, but I'll be there to keep you safe the whole time. And you know what, I'm a little nervous too," said Dad.

"Why?" asked Lily.
"It may be your first time swimming... but it's my first time teaching."

The great thing about Dad was that he was funny.

Even getting changed into their costumes was fun.

You try not to laugh at a grown-up wearing swim shorts on his head!

But they were having a bit too much fun.

When Dad pretended to be a monster and chased Lily to the poolside, the lifeguard told them off! "No running!" he shouted.

Lily and Dad tried not to giggle and walked sensibly (sort of) to the pool steps. Dad helped Lily down the steps.

He waded out in front of her and held out his arms. "OK peanut," he said. "Be brave... swim to me."

Lily took a deep breath... plucked up her courage... and LEAPED into the open water.
She flailed and flapped. She kicked and wriggled.
She SPLISHED and SPLASHED!

But she didn't know what she was doing.
Trying as she was, she was sinking downward, not sailing forward!
Water flowed into her mouth. "HELP!" she yelled.
"HEEELLGGGGggggp!"

"Woah, woah!" said Dad, scooping her up.
"You OK?" "COUGH! COUGH! SPLUTTER!" Lily caught her breath.
"Yes!" she finally managed to say. "I'm OK."
"I think we need to start with something easier, don't you?" asked Dad.
"I do!" said Lily.

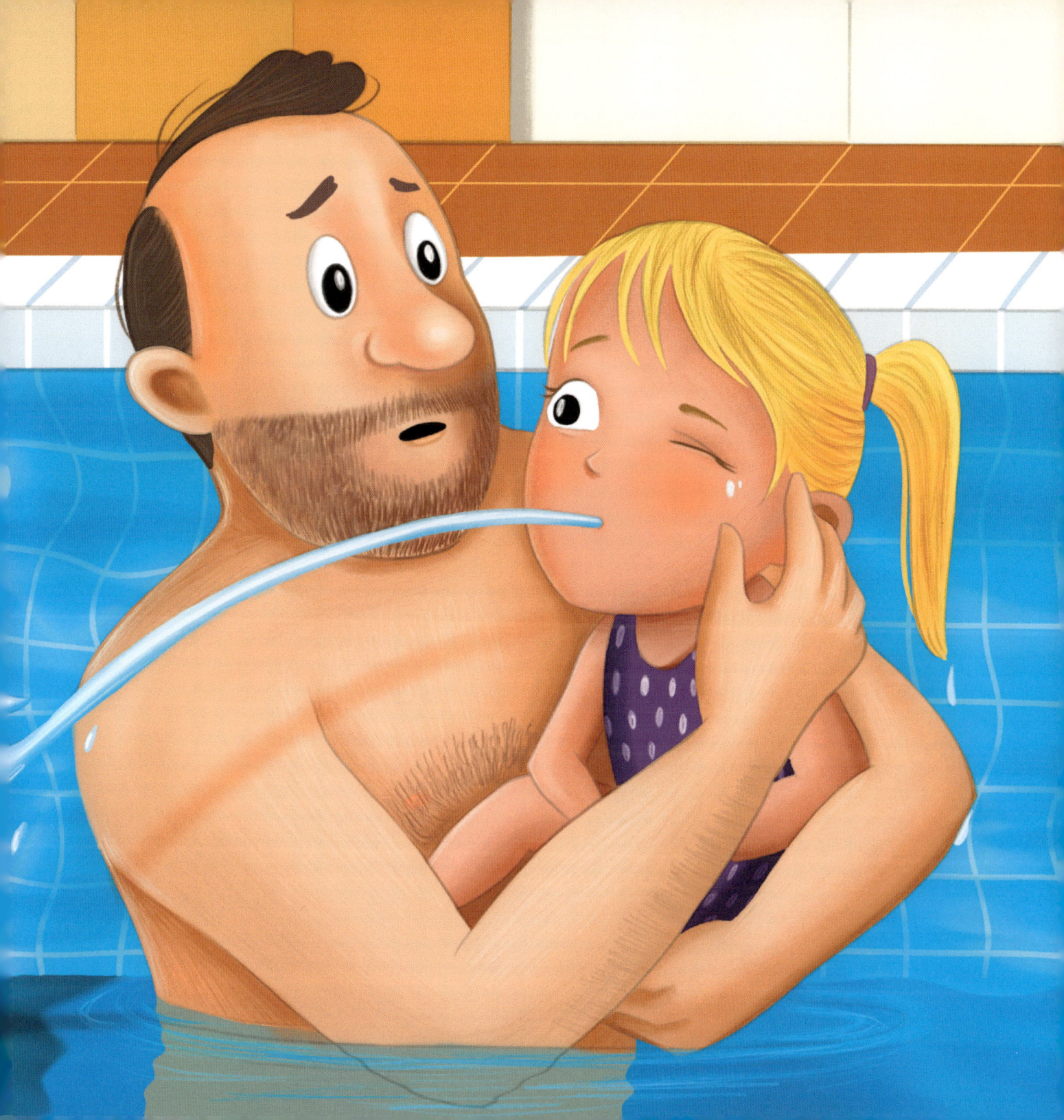

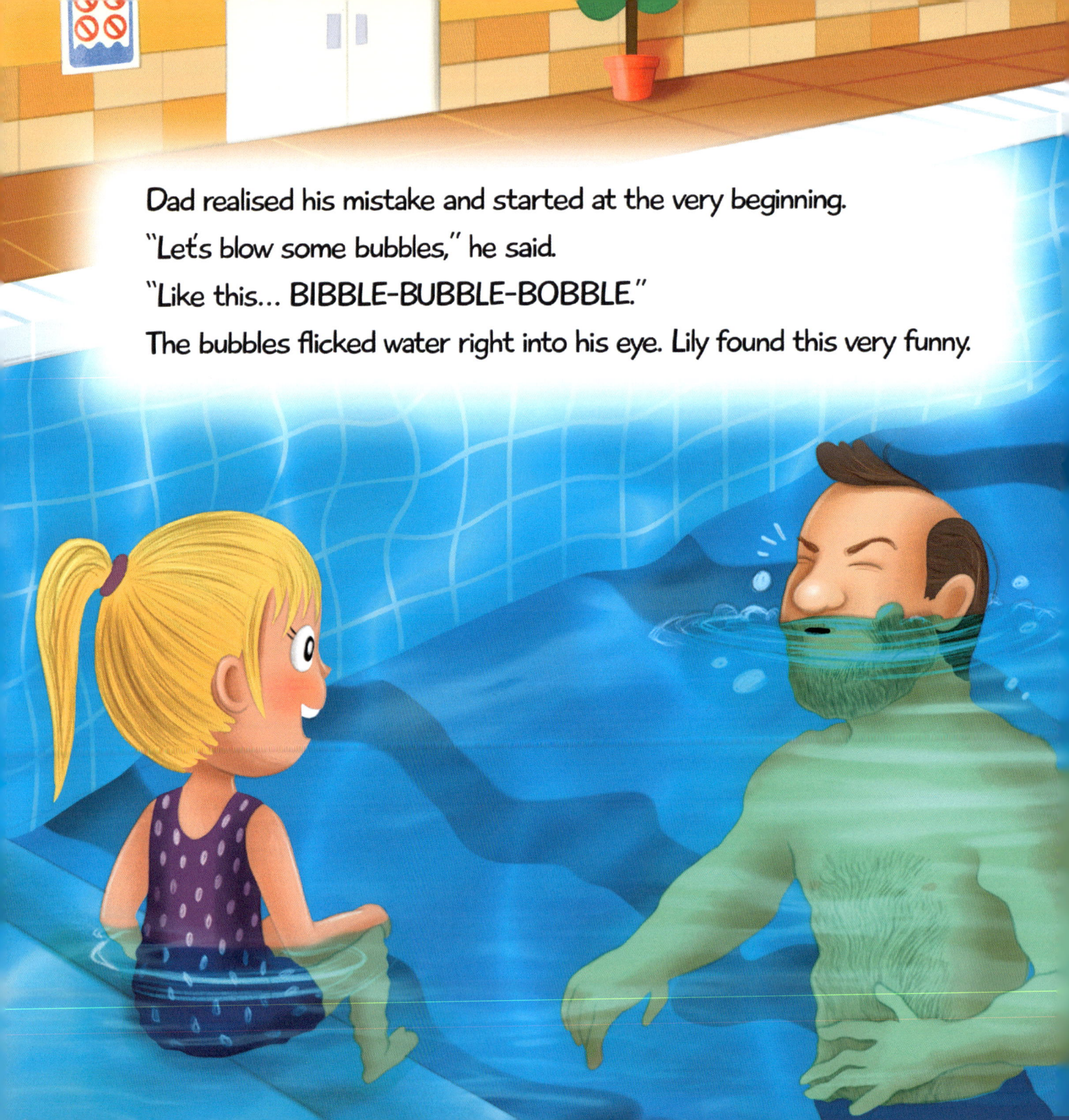

Dad realised his mistake and started at the very beginning.

"Let's blow some bubbles," he said.

"Like this... BIBBLE-BUBBLE-BOBBLE."

The bubbles flicked water right into his eye. Lily found this very funny.

They blew bubbles all morning.

The more Lily blew, the better she got.

The more confident she got. The bigger the bubbles got.

By lunchtime, she was BIBBLE-BUBBLE-BOBBLEing even bigger than Dad!

Week after week they came.
Each time Lily slowly and carefully learned new skills.

Dad got gradually better at teaching.
Lily got gradually better at being brave in the water.

The week after bubbles, Lily learned to float.

The week after that, she learned to put her face in the water.

The week after that, she learned to kick.

The week after THAT, she learned to paddle.

There were many times when Lily felt like she wanted to give up...

like it was too hard...

but thanks to Dad's encouragement, she always kept going.

Before they knew it, they had been coming to the big pool for 6 months! Before they knew it, it was the big day… and Lily was nervous again.

"OK peanut," said Dad, his arms held out. "Let's try this again.
"Be brave… swim to me."
Once more, Lily took a deep breath… plucked up her courage… and **LEAPED** into the open water.

She kicked neatly. She paddled skilfully.
She glided gracefully through the water and safely into Dad's arms.

"You did it!" yelled Dad with glee.
"I did!" replied Lily.
"We did it together!" they said.

Printed in Great Britain
by Amazon